IRIS MURDOCH

IRIS
MURDOCH

by

A. S. BYATT

Edited by Ian Scott-Kilvert

PUBLISHED FOR
THE BRITISH COUNCIL
BY LONGMAN GROUP LTD

LONGMAN GROUP LTD
Longman House, Burnt Mill, Harlow, Essex

*Associated companies, branches and
representatives throughout the world*

First published 1976
ⓒ A. S. Byatt 1976

*Printed in England by
Bradleys, Reading and London*

ISBN 0 582 01252 X

IRIS MURDOCH

I

IRIS MURDOCH's achievement as a novelist has frequently seemed problematic to critics, reviewers and even readers, though her books have always sold extremely well, both in Britain and in other countries. When her first novels appeared in the mid 1950s, she was immediately classed with the 'Angry Young Men', for reasons now hard to discern, since she was certainly not angry and was interested much more in philosophical games and in the nature of fiction itself than in social protest (although she had been a Marxist, and had worked with the war refugees in camps for Displaced Persons). What she had then in common with writers like Kingsley Amis and John Wain was an interest in rapid comedy, and the long English tradition of the farcical episodic novel, though in fact, even then, her work was much more closely related to that of Beckett and the French existentialists and surrealists than to the eighteenth-century comic novels which Amis and Wain admired. Later, whilst she herself was claiming that she was 'a realist', and a novelist in the English realist tradition as exemplified by Jane Austen, George Eliot and E. M. Forster, academic critics were, with some justification, elucidating her novels as elaborate reconstructions of Celtic fertility myths (*A Severed Head*) or Freudian kingship (*The Unicorn*). There is a large and flourishing academic community of Iris Murdoch students, and there is a large number of suspicious reviewers and readers who find the elaborate, in some ways intensely artificial, world of her novels difficult to take. She is accused at once of being mandarin and sensational. She is described as the heir to the liberal humanism and technical subtlety of E. M. Forster, and at the same time compared, with some justice, to best-selling writers of melodrama (Daphne du Maurier), or detective stories for lady dons. (There is certainly something recognizably akin to the Murdoch world in the fantastic, busy, contrived, yet emotionally pleasing world of Margery Allingham's detective stories.) There is a perpetual debate about the probability, or improbability of Miss Murdoch's plots, centring largely on her characters' sexual behaviour. Her characters fall in love, fall in and out of bed, across barriers of age and sex normally assumed to be impassable, even break the incest tabu, with a kind of dance-like formalized frequency which some critics find fascinating, and indeed lifelike, some irritating, and some to have deep cultural or ritual symbolic meaning. (All three responses may, and do, occur at once in some readers.) I hope, at least, in what follows, to elucidate some of the ideas, about life and about fiction, behind the construction of this world, and then to return to the question of its success.

II

Iris Murdoch is a philosopher as well as a novelist. Her philosophical work deals largely with the relations between art and morals, both of which she sees as, at their best, sustained attempts to distinguish truth from fantasy, particularly in the presentation of a sufficiently complex image of the human personality, and to find out what we mean by, what we really hold to be, 'Good'. It seems to me that the relationship between the kind of conceptual thought and the kind of fiction she writes has been unusually fruitful, very much part of the same search for ways of understanding, both historically and practically, the way human beings work. It seems therefore, a good way to begin a discussion of her novels by mapping out some of her ideas.

Perhaps her best-known piece of conceptual writing is 'Against Dryness', published in 1961 in *Encounter*, in which she argued that one of the major problems of the modern novel is that after two wars, and the philosophical debates of the Enlightenment, Romanticism and the Liberal tradition, 'we have been left with far too shallow and flimsy a view of human personality'. Briefly, she distinguishes between two archetypal modern ideas of man. Ordinary Language Man, as exemplified in the works of modern English linguistic philosophers,[1] characteristically sees himself as

rational and totally free except in so far as—in the most ordinary law-court and commonsensical sense—his degree of self-awareness may vary. He is morally speaking monarch of all he surveys and totally responsible for his actions. Nothing transcends him. His moral language is a practical pointer, the instrument of his choices, the indication of his preferences . . . His moral arguments are references to empirical facts backed up by decisions. The only moral word he requires is 'good' (or 'right') the word which expresses decision . . . The virtue which is fundamental to him is sincerity.

('Against Dryness', p. 17)

The alternative image of human nature is Totalitarian Man, particularly exemplified in the works of Sartre and the French existentialists. This Man feels anguish, or *Angst*, in the face of an absurd or hostile universe. His highest value is his own will, his own assertion of his solitary self, against a society suffering from an absence of God and its own hypocrisy and pointlessness. Again, Totalitarian Man's major virtue is sincerity, that is, a scrupulous attention to presenting himself as he sees himself. Miss Murdoch feels that both these images of the human self are profoundly inadequate, partly because they are egoistic, partly because they do not allow for the *variety* of experience, of men, of language, which human beings in practice encounter. She attempts to reassert the implicit and explicit values of the great nineteenth-century novelists who (partly because nineteenth-century society was dynamic and interesting) were more interested in the precise details of life, and the relation to these of complexities of thought. She writes, in 'Against Dryness', in prose of true eloquence:

What have we lost here? And what have we perhaps never had? We have suffered a general loss of concepts, the loss of a moral and political vocabulary. We no longer use a spread-out substantial picture of the manifold virtues of man and society.

[1] I take these to be the philosophers who have learned from Wittgenstein, such as Gilbert Ryle, and The Logical Positivists, such as A. J. Ayer. The particular example Miss Murdoch offers in 'Against Dryness' is drawn from Stuart Hampshire's *Thought and Action*.

We no longer see man against a background of values, of realities, which transcend him. We picture man as a brave naked will surrounded by an easily comprehended empirical world. For the hard idea of truth we have substituted a facile idea of sincerity. What we have never had, of course, is a satisfactory Liberal theory of personality, a theory of man as free and separate and related to a rich and complicated world from which, as a moral being, he has much to learn.

(ibid., p. 18)

In other philosophical essays, particularly 'The Sublime and the Beautiful Revisited' and 'The Sublime and the Good', Iris Murdoch attempts to be more precise about the processes by which we, historically and personally, arrive at experiences of freedom, or virtue, or beauty. She wrote in 1970 'When I was young I thought, as all young people do, that freedom was the thing. Later on I felt that virtue was the thing. Now I begin to suspect that freedom and virtue are concepts which ought to be pinned into place by some more fundamental thinking about a proper quality of human life, which *begins* at the food and shelter level'.[1] In her book on Sartre she is much concerned with limiting and defining his notions of freedom, both in art and in politics. In 'The Sublime and the Beautiful Revisited' she comes to define freedom and virtue as in some ways identical—and they are related to beauty, too, because they are related to the kind of *formal* truth-seeking of the artist.

Virtue is not essentially or immediately concerned with choosing between actions or rules or reasons, nor with stripping the personality for a leap. It is concerned with really apprehending that other people exist. This too is what freedom really is; and it is impossible not to feel the creation of a work of art as a struggle for freedom. Freedom is not choosing; that is merely the move that we make when all is already lost. Freedom is knowing and understanding and respecting things quite other than ourselves. Virtue is in this sense to be construed as knowledge and connects us so with reality.

('The Sublime and the Beautiful Revisited', pp. 269–70)

[1] 'Existentialists and Mystics', p. 179. See Bibliography, p. 40.

One of the moral and aesthetic terms to which Iris Murdoch most frequently returns is 'attention'. 'Attention' is a word used by Simone Weil to describe the constantly renewed attempt to see things, objects, people, moral situations, truly as they are, uncoloured by our own personal fantasies or needs for consolation. Attention is in this sense a willed, thoughtful, selfless contemplation: Simone Weil remarks that those who *attend* properly to life make their moral decisions in terms of what their attention has made of them. They are not free to make random leaps of faith or violence; the freedom was in the choice of attending in the first place. In Miss Murdoch's thought, such attention is connected to Kant's concept of *Achtung* (attention) or respect for the moral law, which is 'a kind of suffering pride which accompanies, though it does not motivate, the recognition of duty. It is an actual experience of freedom (akin to the existentialist *Angst*), the realization that although swayed by passions we are also capable of rational conduct.' It is such attention which causes Miss Murdoch in 'On "God" and "Good"'[1] to be able to write 'Freedom is not strictly the exercise of the will, but rather the experience of accurate vision which, when this becomes appropriate, occasions action'.

The concept of attention in Miss Murdoch's terms is closely related to the concept of good, or goodness. Throughout her philosophical writings she returns to the question of perfection, of the nature of truth, of whether there can be said or seen to be any transcendent good outside human imperfections and vanities, in some way beyond the operations of time, chance and necessity, which can be a meaningful object of contemplation. In 'The Idea of Perfection' she criticizes the critics of G. E. Moore. Moore believed that 'good was a supersensible reality, that it was a mysterious quality . . . that it was an object of knowledge and (implicitly) that to be able to see it was in some sense to have it. He thought of the good upon the analogy of the beautiful . . .'. Moore's critics (especially Ordinary Language Man) thought 'good' was a subjective value-judgement, 'a movable label affixed to the world', not 'an object of insight or knowledge but a function

[1] In *The Sovereignty of Good*, p. 67.

of the will'. Miss Murdoch said she agreed almost entirely with Moore, and not with his critics.[1]

Miss Murdoch's own discussions of the process of attention to moral (and aesthetic) goodness are conducted with the assumption that such attention will bring with it a sense of where goodness and truth and reality *are*, that they are neither subjective nor arbitrarily open to the election of the will. Her most powerful discussions of the term 'attention' use in primary moral ways words which have become part of the technical language of literary criticism: realism, fantasy, naturalism. For instance:

I would suggest that the authority of the Good seems to us something necessary because the realism (ability to perceive reality) required for goodness is a kind of intellectual ability to perceive what is true, which is automatically at the same time a suppression of self. *The necessity of the good is then an aspect of the kind of necessity involved in any technique for exhibiting fact.*

('On "God" and "Good",' p. 66)

Or, from the same essay, a little earlier:

One might start from the assertion that morality, goodness, is a form of realism. The idea of a really good man living in a private dream world seems unacceptable. Of course a good man may be infinitely eccentric but he must know certain things about his surroundings, most obviously the existence of other people and their claims. The chief enemy of excellence in morality (and also in art) is personal fantasy: the tissue of self-aggrandizing and consoling wishes and dreams which prevents one from seeing what is there outside one. Rilke said of Cézanne that he did not paint 'I like it', he painted 'There it is'. This is not easy and requires, in art or morals, a discipline. One might say here that art is an excellent analogy of morals, or indeed that it is in this respect a case of morals. We cease to be in order to attend to the existence of something else, a natural object, a person in need. We can see in mediocre art, where perhaps it is even more clearly seen than in mediocre conduct, the intrusion of fantasy, the assertion of self, the dimming of any reflection of the real world.

(ibid., p. 59)

---

[1] 'The Idea of Perfection', in *The Sovereignty of Good*, pp. 3–4.

In terms of the relationship between aesthetics and morals. Miss Murdoch's descriptions of the objects of fictional attention are instructive. She claims that true 'goodness', almost impossible to be clear about in life, can be discerned in art, that we can build an aesthetic, and a moral vision, from attempting to understand the precise nature of the excellence of Tolstoy, or, above all, Shakespeare. To these great writers she ascribes a quality which she initially names 'tolerance' or 'agnosticism'—related both to Simone Weil's impersonal 'attention' and to Keats's 'negative capability'.[1] To this quality she later gives the name, love. She writes

Art and morals are, with certain provisos . . . one. Their essence is the same. The essence of both of them is love. Love is the perception of individuals. Love is the extremely difficult realisation that something other than oneself is real. Love, and so art and morals, is the discovery of reality. What stuns us into a realisation of our supersensible destiny is not, as Kant imagined, the formlessness of nature but rather its unutterable particularity; and most particular and individual of all natural things is the mind of man.

('The Sublime and the Good', p. 51)

The unutterable particularity, of experience in general, and of individual human beings in particular, is something to which, both as philosopher and novelist, she returns again and again. 'Against Dryness' ends with a plea to modern novelists, and modern Liberals of all kinds, to avoid simplified theories, Marxist or Existentialist, which assume that 'reality is a given whole', that there can be a theory which immutably describes our world. We must, she says, respect contingency and learn a new respect for the particularity of 'the now so unfashionable naturalistic idea of character'. 'Contingency' is a crucial and recurring word in Miss Murdoch's philosophical writings, and indeed in her novels also. It is used to describe what is random, accidental, simply factual, about things and people—what is both immediate, and not part of any formal plan or pattern.

[1] 'Negative capability' is a phrase used by Keats in a letter to describe the particular quality of Shakespeare's imagination—the capacity not to formulate ideas or patterns but to be 'capable of being in uncertainties, mysteries, doubts, without any irritable reaching after fact and reason'.

Real people are destructive of myth, contingency is destructive of fantasy and opens the way for imagination. Think of the Russians, those great masters of the contingent. Too much contingency of course may turn art into journalism. But since reality is incomplete, art must not be too much afraid of incompleteness. Literature must always represent a battle between real people and images; and what it requires now is a much stronger and more complex conception of the former.

('Against Dryness', p. 20)

There is a great deal of tough thought behind these generalizations, these definitions of concepts. The same qualities of moral toughness and intellectual decisiveness have led Iris Murdoch to be able to make some precise and imaginative generalizations about the state of modern fiction, and its relation to the fiction of earlier times. It should by now be clear that Miss Murdoch prefers the major nineteenth-century novels, on grounds both moral and aesthetic, to twentieth-century ones. In 'Against Dryness' she offers a brilliant description of the modern novel as either 'crystalline' or 'journalistic'. The crystalline novel is 'a small quasi-allegorical object portraying the human condition and not containing "characters" in the nineteenth-century sense'.[1] It is related to Symbolism and symbolic form, it sees a novel as an *object*. The journalistic work is a 'large shapeless quasi-documentary object, the degenerate descendant of the 19th-century novel'. Both of these relate to the impoverished images of human nature I described earlier. Totalitarian Man is interested in the Human Condition, not the messy particular individual. His art is the crystalline work with himself as symbolic representative of mankind. Ordinary Language Man produces documents, concerned with social facts of behaviour, eschewing metaphysical depths.

In a later essay 'Existentialists and Mystics' Miss Murdoch created another dichotomy, between the existential novel and

---

[1] Examples of the crystalline novel might be French philosophical myths like Sartre's *La Nausée* or Camus's *La Chute* (*The Fall*), or in English some of the elegant, beautifully shaped late fables of Muriel Spark—*The Driver's Seat*, *The Public Image*—or William Golding's *Pincher Martin*, an allegorized vision of a man coming to grips with his death. Much good recent American fiction, such as that of Thomas Pynchon, is also 'crystalline' in form.

the mystical novel. The existential novel derives from Romanticism, like Totalitarian man: it believes in the individual will and vision, in a society where there are no longer political or religious certainties to give automatic depth to a picture. It is 'the story of the lonely brave man, defiant without optimism, proud without pretension, always an exposer of shams, whose mode of being is a deep criticism of society. He is an adventurer. He is godless. He does not suffer from guilt. He thinks of himself as free . . .' (D. H. Lawrence, Hemingway, Camus, Sartre). The mystical novel tries to return to the concept of God, or good, or virtue, and has to invent its own religious images in an empty situation (Greene, White, Bellow, Spark, Golding). Miss Murdoch claims that the new generation, concerned with human needs, now always present to our consciousness, for food, shelter, survival, is in fact utilitarian in that it works, morally, spiritually, up and out from biological survival. And this utilitarianism is a form of *naturalism*, she says, and implies that this naturalism could possibly create an aesthetic of its own, with stories in which goodness will be seen to be empirically necessary, particular, subject to chance and necessity, but valuable. The particularity of this new naturalism could not be the particularity of Tolstoy or George Eliot, because they were working and observing human beings in a world where there was a strong consensus about the nature of religion, society, politics, duty, whether one chose to elaborate or contradict this consensus. But, Miss Murdoch claims, art has always presented recognizable images of human value or virtue which survive social and metaphysical upheavals (the kindness of Patroclus or Alyosha, the truthfulness of Cordelia and Mr Knightley).[1]

One last word about Miss Murdoch's general ideas about art and life, before I proceed to a particular discussion of her fiction. She is a writer with a powerful sense of the difficulties entailed by any process of formulation in our attempts to attend to reality. She opens the essay 'Existentialists and Mystics' with a remark on this subject.

Art represents a sort of paradox in human communication.

[1] Patroclus in Homer's *Iliad;* Alyosha in Dostoevsky's *The Brothers Karamazov;* Cordelia in Shakespeare's *King Lear;* Mr Knightley in Jane Austen's *Emma.*

In order to tell the truth, especially about anything complicated, we need a conceptual apparatus which partly has the effect of concealing what it attempts to reveal.

('Existentialists and Mystics', p. 169)

In 'Against Dryness' she was pleading both for 'more concepts in terms of which to picture the substance of our being' and for a suspicion of the forms we *do* use to think, to perceive with. This sense runs through all her works, of a contrary tug of value between attempts at form and attempts to live with the knowledge that 'what *does* exist is brute and nameless, it escapes from the scheme of relations in which we imagine it to be rigidly enclosed, it escapes from language and science, it is more and other than our descriptions of it'.[1]

Her aesthetic remarks about this subject are, I think, both unusually clear and unusually subtle. She has, in her book *Sartre: Romantic Rationalist*, an excellent passage on the problems created by our modern attitude to language. This is impossible, in its admirable suggestiveness and precision, to summarize, but it is concerned with the effect on literature of our *self-consciousness* (historically exacerbated by the advent of scientific method, scientific symbolic languages), about the relationship between words and things. We know our language, both descriptive and emotive, creates the way we see things and also can be changed, is relative, if we use other concepts, other languages. So we think *about* words, as well as thinking *with* words. We are, says Miss Murdoch 'like people who for a long time looked out of a window without noticing the glass—and then one day began to notice this too'. We began to question the *nature* of referential language, which produced phenomena like Sartre's hero's nausea at the fact that the word *tree* bore no relation to the thing he saw, or, alternatively, Mallarmé's attempts to make language self-referring, abstract, like paint, like music.

As Miss Murdoch says, the novel is naturally 'referential' because it tells a story, and 'the telling of a story seems to demand a discursive referential use of language to describe one event after another. The novelist seemed to be, by profession, more deeply rooted in the ordinary world where things were still things and words were still their names.'

[1] *Sartre: Romantic Rationalist*, ch. i.

But the novel, too, has become (in ways she defines in *Sartre*) linguistically self-conscious.[1]

Miss Murdoch's call for more and better defined moral concepts, on one hand, and her passionate belief in the importance of *stories*, of primitive human recounting of events, seem to me to be important ways of dealing with this problem. In 'The Idea of Perfection' she tells the story of the moral process whereby a mother-in-law comes to attend to the reality of a daughter-in-law she doesn't like, realizing that she is not 'vulgar' but 'refreshingly simple' and so on. This story is a novel in little: it also requires that reader and character *use* the conceptual words involved. Miss Murdoch says of this example 'I drew attention to the important part played by the normative-descriptive words, the specialised or secondary value words (such as "vulgar", "spontaneous" etc.). By means of these words there takes place what we might call "the siege of the individual by concepts". Uses of such words are both instruments and symptoms of learning.'

In an article on T. S. Eliot as moralist Iris Murdoch praises Eliot both for asserting the impersonality of the artist and for 'a continual concern, in the midst of difficulties, for the referential character of words'. T. S. Eliot has never 'made war upon language' and this is good.[2]

Shifting language, shifting concepts, never adequate, continually to be re-established and modified. Miss Murdoch makes Lawrentian claims for the importance of the novelist. 'The writer has always been important, and is now *essential*, as a truth-teller and as a defender of words. (There is only one culture and words are its basis.)' She sees the primitive force of stories, as a way of preserving, against our self-questioning, our culture and our language. 'The story is almost as funda-mental a human concept as the thing, and however much novelists may try, for reasons of fashion or art, to stop telling stories, the story is always likely to break out again in a new form. Everything else may be done by pictures or computers, but stories about human beings are best told in words, and that "best" is a matter of a response to a deep and ordinary human need.'

[1] *Sartre: Romantic Rationalist*, ch. iii.
[2] 'T. S. Eliot as a Moralist', p. 156.

Truth, the preservation of language, stories. But although *the novelist is potentially the greatest truth-teller of them all*, he is also an expert fantasy-monger'.[1] Throughout Miss Murdoch's work runs a warning against the consolations of form.

Tragedy in art is the attempt to overcome the defeat which human beings suffer in the practical world. It is, as Kant nearly said, as he ought to have said, the human spirit mourning and yet exulting in its strength. In the practical world there may be only mourning and the final acceptance of the incomplete. Form is the great consolation of love, but it is also its great temptation.

('The Sublime and the Good', p. 55)

III

Iris Murdoch is now the author of seventeen novels. It is clearly not possible to discuss all of them in detail. What I propose to attempt is to group the novels in terms of the technical and philosophical preoccupations which seem to have been paramount in the writing of them.

The first two novels, *Under the Net* and *The Flight from the Enchanter* differ from all the later ones in various obvious ways. Formally, they could both be classified as 'fantasy-myth' in Miss Murdoch's own terms, and are akin to Beckett's *Murphy* and still more, Raymond Queneau's *Pierrot mon Ami*, a gentle surrealist picaresque fantasy. (Both *Murphy* and *Pierrot* are in Jake's library in *Under the Net*, which is dedicated to Queneau). Both are philosophical fables, using a proliferation of characters and dramatic incidents, farcical or tragic, to illustrate a central theme. In *Under the Net* that theme is the one to which I have just referred, the necessity and danger of concepts, forms, in thought and action, both in the worlds of art, of politics, of work, of morals and of love. In *The Flight from the Enchanter* the theme is social, and concerns the proper and improper uses of power, personal and public, playing comic and bitter

---

[1] 'Existentialists and Mystics', p. 182.

games with various forms of enslavement and emancipation, sexual, financial, bureaucratic, military. Both novels are close to Miss Murdoch's work on Sartre, in the sense that, lightly but profoundly, they take up the Sartrean issues, the relationship of the individual, and of art, to political structures and ideals, the nature of freedom, the nature of language. The central figures of both works, Jake Donaghue and Rosa Keepe are Sartrean in the sense that they 'move through a society which [Sartre's man] finds unreal and alien but without the consolation of a rational universe. His action seems not to lie *in* this social world; his freedom is a mysterious point which he is never sure of having reached. His virtue lies in understanding his own contingency in order to assume it, not the contingency of the world in order to alter it. It seems as if what 'justifies' him is just this precarious honesty, haunted as it is by a sense of the absolute.' Sartre's heroes, Miss Murdoch says, are 'anti-totalitarian and anti-bourgeois'. Jake is certainly both—he won't write socialist propaganda for Lefty Todd, he won't, equally, attach himself more than peripherally to the capitalist world of bookmakers, film-makers and money-makers whom he occasionally cynically exploits. Rosa, aware of the faults of the Welfare State diagnosed in 'Against Dryness', aware that modern liberalism is not enough, although descended from a family of battling reformers and suffragettes, has retreated into a kind of stultified identification with the oppressed and is operating a mindless machine in a factory. She is floating and unrelated. 'She had ceased to imagine that her life would ever consist of anything but a series of interludes.' 'Where beauty and goodness were concerned, Rosa had, of course, no particular expectations from her new life.'

I want to leave consideration of *Under the Net* to a later point, but it might at this point be worth going in further detail into the relationship between thought and form in *The Flight from the Enchanter*. This novel puzzled reviewers and irritated critics, who tended pompously to castigate it for failures in realism of a kind it was not attempting, or like F. R. Karl for 'creating characters who are suitable only for the comic situations but for little else'.[1] In fact the power of

[1] F. R. Karl, *The Contemporary English Novel*, London 1963, p. 261.

this novel lies in the intricate patterning of its variations on a theme which, however comically treated, is shown to the *mind* to have tragic implications.

It is a novel about the rootlessness caused by the second World War, and is full of refugees and persons without political identity—from Nina, the dressmaker, the archetypal victim first of violence, then of bureaucracy, finally of Rosa's obsession with her own fantasies of enchantment, to Annette who is rich, young, emotional and in a sense untouchable. Miss Murdoch, besides her interest in the fate of Liberalism, is an admirer of Simone Weil, whose studies of 'affliction', in communities or individuals, contributed much to the depth of this book. Simone Weil was interested in the mechanical way in which the suffering was transferred from person to person, a blow was passed on, the damaged attracted violence and in their turn inflicted damage. Uprooted central European refugees, the Lusiewicz brothers, Mischa Fox, provide the daemonic forces of enslavement, loose unconnected power, both in the fairy-tale, in the sexual, and in the social areas of this work. The novel is pervaded by images of traps and hunts, machines which savage their slaves (Nina's sewing-machine, Calvin Blick's camera), fish and underwater guns. Sexuality is seen largely in terms of enchantment, pursuit of a free creature, enslavement of a free creature. (Rainborough has fantasies of Annette as a smooth little fish, 'graceful, mysterious, desirable and free—and the next moment there is only struggling and blood and confusion. If only, he thought, it were possible to combine the joys of contemplation and possession.')

Mischa Fox, at a much more extreme point, is caught in the same paradox. Obsessed by suffering, caught in its machinery, he sees power as protection, and protection paradoxically leads to destruction; he is compelled to destroy what he protects, from chickens, to 'slaves', to women. His battle to gain possession of the suffragette periodical, the *Artemis* (named itself after the virgin huntress, edited by Rosa's brother, Hunter Keepe, his name the paradox of pursuit and possession in little) typifies both political and sexual themes. A central moment of the novel is the wildly funny scene in which the elderly suffragettes frustrate the bid to assimilate the paper to Fox's empire. An old lady says:

'Why the very fact that "female emancipation" still has meaning for us proves that it has not yet been achieved.'

Calvin . . . said suddenly, 'Would you agree, Madam, that the fact that the phrase "emancipation of the serfs" is significant, proves that the serfs are not yet emancipated?'

This book is a precisely light testimony to Miss Murdoch's knowledge that *neither* are emancipated—and that our own society has not got the will and the means to see or deal with this.

If these early novels ask Sartrean questions, they do not offer Sartrean answers. Sartre's heroes agonize and contemplate in a lucidly tortured solitude. Miss Murdoch points out that Sartre claimed that 'the mode of self-awareness of the modern novelist is the internal monologue', which is not primarily concerned with 'character' and 'individuality' in either the narrating consciousness or the other people reflected through it. She criticizes his novels, further, for not presenting individuals in the world of action.

Sartre's individual is neither the socially integrated hero of Marxism nor the full-blooded romantic hero who believes in the reality and importance of his personal struggle. For Sartre the 'I' is always unreal. The real individual is Ivich [the silent sister in *Les Chemins de la Liberté*] opaque, sinister, unintelligible and irreducibly other; seen always from outside . . . Sartre, like Freud, sees life as an egocentric drama.

(*Sartre, Romantic Rationalist*, ch. VII, VIII)

There is a sense in which the comic and densely populated worlds of Iris Murdoch's first two fantasies are a kind of meaningful game with the Sartrean universe. Jake tries an internal monologue, but discovers that the world is full of other people whose views he has misinterpreted but *can learn*. Rosa fails to observe properly the individual life and needs of Nina—but they are there *to be observed*, and Rosa can learn. No single view of the world, no one vision, is shown to be adequate, in a form of novel where everyone is always offering epigrammatic views on the nature of society or reality or suffering. No one is right, but everyone—Dave Gellman, the linguistic philosopher, Lefty Todd, the socialist, Rainborough, the mediocre modern élite bureaucrat—is there, and reader and other characters must take them into account. I have described elsewhere how I think the last scene of *Under the Net* is a comic parody of the end of *La Nausée*.[1] Both Jake and Roquentin are saved from a sense of futility and drudgery by a vision of their future induced by hearing a song. But Roquentin turns *from* the nauseating horrors of the world and society to the pure necessity of art. Jake finds a way into curiosity about, and delight in, the endless differences of people and proliferation of things. It is the villain of *The Flight from the Enchanter*, Calvin Blick, who offers the solipsist view, to Rosa, that 'You will never know the truth and you will read the signs in accordance with your own deepest wishes. That is what we human beings always have to do. Reality is a cipher with many solutions, all of them right ones'.

This is not so: no solution is complete, but some are wrong, and freedom consists in *not* reading the signs according to personal fantasy or desire. And this can be done. The sense that the characters in these books have reached new insights and new beginnings is worked for, and valuable.

Miss Murdoch also wrote of Sartre that he had 'an impatience, which is fatal to a novelist proper, with the *stuff* of human life'. He has an interest in the details of contemporary living, and a passionate desire to analyse and 'build intellectually pleasing schemes and patterns. But the feature which might enable these two talents to fuse into the work of a great novelist is absent, namely an apprehension of the absurd irreducible uniqueness of people and of their relations with each other.'[2] Her next book, *The Sandcastle*, is dedicated to her husband, John Bayley, and her work from *The Sandcastle* onwards shows an increasing concern with the moral and critical principles explored in his book, *The Characters of Love*, and later in *Tolstoy and the Novel*. John Bayley argues that the contemporary impatience with the

[1] See A. S. Byatt, *Degrees of Freedom*, London 1965.
[2] *Sartre: Romantic Rationalist*, ch. x.

idea of 'character' as an attempt to create a unique individual is a sign both of a literary and of a moral failing. Both he and Iris Murdoch quote with approval Henry James on Balzac's characters—'it was by loving them that he knew them, not by knowing them that he loved'. Both see it as a function of the English novel at its greatest that the writers, and thus the readers, *loved* the characters and felt them to be free agents, in some sense. Both are troubled at the erosion of the sense of reality of characters created by insistent aesthetic symbolism in novels, or by the attempt to write allegories of the Human Condition. Iris Murdoch's technical interest in nineteenth-century 'realism' is an interest in the recreation of a fictional world in which separate individuals meet, change, communicate. A good novel is 'a house fit for free characters to live in'. Before *The Sandcastle* Miss Murdoch's models were French, or Irish; now she makes a sustained effort, in *The Sandcastle*, *The Bell*, *An Unofficial Rose*, to learn from Jane Austen, George Eliot, Henry James.

The Sandcastle is a not entirely successful attempt at a description of a 'normal' but difficult moral problem—the attempt by Mor, a middle-aged schoolmaster, to break out of a largely dead marriage when he falls in love with a young woman painter, Rain Carter. It contains a character—Bledyard, the art master—who combines T. S. Eliot's view of the impersonality of the artist, with John Bayley's sense that the individual human being is a mystery, a compelling moral object, incredibly difficult to comprehend. He argues that the true artist 'is humble enough in the presence of the object to attempt *merely* to show what the object is like. But this *merely*, in painting, is everything.' And he asks 'who can look reverently enough upon another human face?'

Bledyard argues further that Mor, planning a violent bid for freedom, is indulging in fantasy. 'You do not truly apprehend the distinct being of either your wife or Miss Carter.' In *The Bell* and in *An Unofficial Rose* Iris Murdoch makes much more successful and sustained attempts at showing efforts, failures, partial failures, to apprehend the distinct being of other people.

Both *The Bell* and *An Unofficial Rose* are concerned with the relationships between freedom and virtue, and also between beauty and truth. Both could be described, as *Howard's End* or *A Passage to India* could be described, as English symbolic novels, in which a powerful formal element is provided by the relationship of plot and characters to certain symbolic objects.

In *The Bell* the central episodes of the plot concern the substitution of the medieval bell (legendarily supposed to have flown from the Abbey belfry into the lake when a nun had a lover) for the new bell, decked to enter the Abbey as a bride, or postulant, and open a new kind of speech between the enclosed, silent religious order and the outside world. The bell represents art—it is engraved with characters from the life of Christ, who are Iris Murdoch's real other people— 'squat figures—solid, simple, beautiful, absurd, full to the brim with something which was to the artist not an object of speculation or imagination'. As art, it is related to all the other music in the novel, jazz records (primitive sexual urgency), Bach, the 'hideous purity' of the nuns' plainsong, birdsong which to Kant was the only pure because the only free music, natural without concepts. It is also related to the other works of art seen by Dora in a vision in the National Gallery, a moment of truth where Gainsborough's portrait of his children is an image of Iris Murdoch's idea of the recognizable authority of the Good. The central symbols in *An Unofficial Rose* are analogous. They are, first, the Tintoretto portrait of Susannah, golden, serene, authoritative, a source of power and value, both moral, aesthetic and social (it is sold, for a large sum, to purchase a fantasy of freedom for Randall, a freedom in itself an enslavement to a factitious beauty). And second, the rose itself, like the birdsong a *natural* beauty, with a *natural* form, also, on a rose farm, a source of value, vision, or even money. Both novels are about the intermittent human attempts to reach perfection, vision, a life which shall seem to have a sense of form or destiny. Both describe a large number of patterned, related, individual successes and failures. Both, also, like *Under the Net* and some later books, are about the pull between silence as purity, and the use of language as a necessary means to discovery of truth and complexity. What is most impressive about both is the degree to which Miss Murdoch succeeds in her aim of creating free and individual characters, whose experience is diverse and not to be summed up.

In 'The Sublime and the Beautiful Revisited' Iris Murdoch makes a very useful distinction between what she calls 'convention' and 'neurosis', which are, she explains, 'the two enemies of understanding, one might say the enemies of love; and how difficult it is in the modern world to escape from one without invoking the help of the other'. 'Convention' is the force which drives Ordinary Language Man, who believes that moral issues are simple—there are rules, and choices, and an existing decorum made by a civilized society. 'Neurosis' drives Totalitarian man who sees the world, and his life, as a dramatic myth, who requires his life to have an absolute form and purpose. In the delicate and detailed descriptions of the moral decisions of the principal characters in *The Bell* and *An Unofficial Rose* we can see the effort, reasoned or instinctive, to understand and love, falling away constantly into one or the other. Neurosis drives Randall, who leaves his wife to suffer enslavement at the hands of Lindsay Rimmer; while Lindsay herself, an earthly Venus, not a heavenly one, is the slave of Emma Sands who writes detective stories with structured plots, and whom Randall's father, Hugh, rejected, for no clear reason, in order to stay with his wife. Randall leaves the natural roses to be 'a writer', for form—and ends up living off his father's sale of the Tintoretto in an empty freedom designed, he suspects, as part of Emma's vengeance. Convention drives his father, Hugh, who could not leave his wife. It drives, supremely, Randall's wife, Ann, the 'unofficial rose' of the title, who is in love with Felix, a soldier and a gentleman, also held by convention, and who is unable to distress her daughter, or abandon the faithless Randall, for happiness against duty.

In *The Bell* it is Michael Meade, homosexual schoolmaster, who—with his sense of destiny in his call to the priesthood, his sense of patterns and portents in his life, his imaginative vision of moral situations when he falls in love with Nick as a boy, or impulsively kisses Toby—is tempted towards a neurotic vision (although he ironically fails Nick by a contrary recoil into self-protective convention). Convention is represented by James Tayper Pace who finds it easy to say that some things are *simply* forbidden, and to close a moral argument. There is not space here to describe the patience with which Miss Murdoch explores the fluctuations between vision, convention, neurosis, fantasy in these characters. But it is worth remarking that the fates of the most important—Hugh and Ann in *An Unofficial Rose*, Michael and Dora in *The Bell* are unpredictable precisely because several outcomes are possible to their dilemmas; they are, in other words, 'free' characters. And this is no mean achievement.

In *The Characters of Love* John Bayley, analysing James's *The Golden Bowl*, describes Maggie's love of the Prince as a saving use of convention—she avoids drama, avoids knowledge even, she 'finds in the refuge of convention and deliberate "ignorance" salvation both for herself and for the others'. I have always felt that Ann in *An Unofficial Rose*, whom Randall hates for 'living by rules', who seems to attract suffering, who feels herself 'shapeless and awkward', is related to Maggie, who is mysterious in the way in which 'to be human is to be virtually unknown' and of whom it might be said 'the conventional and the mysterious are closely allied, are indeed one and the same thing.'[1] She is also related to Lionel Trilling's description of Fanny Price in *Mansfield Park* as one who is 'poor in spirit' and thus blessed.[2] One feels, with these early 'realistic' novels of Miss Murdoch, that much of her hope of combining a well-formed novel with a sense of the mystery and formlessness of people's lives has been fulfilled. And it has partly been fulfilled by a profoundly intelligent use of concepts such as convention and neurosis, not as total patterning devices, but as instruments for exploration of character and motive.

Malcolm Bradbury, one of Miss Murdoch's most intelligent critics,[3] has argued that her practice as a novelist in many ways runs counter to her theoretical beliefs. She claims, he says, that life has finally no pattern, no meaning, that we are

[1] John Bayley, *The Characters of Love: A Study in the Literature of Personality*, London 1960, ch. iv.

[2] Lionel Trilling, 'Mansfield Park', in *The Opposing Self*, New York 1955.

[3] See his essay on Iris Murdoch in *Possibilities: Essays on the State of the Novel*, London 1973.

ruled by necessity and chance, yet one of the strengths of both her plotting and her symbolism is that it explores fully the sense in which we feel that our lives *are* gripped by formative forces which function below our conscious knowledge or choice. She describes those aspects of sexual and social behaviour in which men are remarkably similar to each other and meaningful patterns and generalizations can be drawn, whose power can be felt. I refer particularly to the ideas of psychoanalysts and of students of myth, where they are interested not in the individual whole person, but in the machinery of behaviour.

Miss Murdoch frequently uses the word 'machinery' to describe recognizable patterns of human behaviour. In *A Severed Head*, Palmer Anderson, the psychoanalyst, claims that 'The psyche . . . has its own mysterious methods of restoring a balance. It automatically seeks its advantage, its consolation. It is almost entirely a matter of mechanics, and mechanical models are the best to understand it with' (ch. iv). I used to think that this was simply an indication that Palmer was a totalitarian man, unaware of the irreducibly unique individual. I now see that his remark is a statement of a partial truth which interests Iris Murdoch very much. Only unremitting attention to what lies outside the mechanism can save human beings from being entirely controlled by this psychic machinery. Thus Michael Meade is caught in the (excellently described) *machinery* of guilt and repentance. The title of *The Sacred and Profane Love Machine* itself indicates the strength of that novel, which is its exploration of the automatic elements involved in most love, most efforts at virtue, which, imperfectly understood, can grip and destroy. In 'On "God" and "Good" ' Miss Murdoch claims that Freud made an important discovery about the human mind which 'might be called a doctrine of original sin'. This doctrine she describes in this way:

Freud takes a thoroughly pessimistic view of human nature. He sees the psyche as an egocentric system of quasi-mechanical energy, largely determined by its own individual history, whose natural attachments are sexual, ambiguous, and hard for the subject to understand or control. Introspection reveals only the deep tissue of ambivalent motive, and fantasy is a stronger force than reason. Objectivity and unselfishness are not natural to human beings.

('On "God" and "Good",' p. 51)

Later in the same essay she specifically describes a psychic mechanism which has certainly affected her own understanding of behaviour, and played a major part in the plots of her novels.

A chief enemy to such clarity of vision, whether in art or morals, is the system to which the technical name of sado-masochism has been given. It is the peculiar subtlety of this system that, while constantly leading attention and energy back into the self, it can produce, almost all the way as it were to the summit, plausible imitations of what is good. Refined sado-masochism can ruin art which is too good to be ruined by the cruder vulgarities of self-indulgence . . . Fascinating too is the alleged relation of master to slave, of the good self to the bad self . . .

(ibid., p. 68)

There are several novels which one could call 'mythical' novels in which Miss Murdoch's interest in these mechanisms, in parodies of good, in patterning, leads to the structure seeming to hold more aesthetic power than the individual characters—even though the morality of these novels continues to assert the paramount imperative of observing the free individual. Such novels include *A Severed Head*, *The Unicorn*, and *The Time of the Angels*.

The first of these is slightly different from the others, in that it is not concerned with overall metaphysics, but with patterns of social and sexual behaviour. Its cool elegance, its 'dream-like facility' to quote Miss Murdoch on crystalline fantasy-myth, has a bite which comes from observing human helplessness before human incomprehension of the machinery. The central image—the severed head, image of the petrifying Medusa, the dark (female) Celtic gods, the soothsaying Orpheus—has a poetic force that the delicate imagery of Venus and Mars in *Under the Net* for instance, is not required to carry. Alexander, the sculptor of that novel, making a portrait head swathed in bandages, like a death's-head, talks, as Bledyard in *The Sandcastle* talks, of the use of portraiture as a means to truth. But the associations are those of magic, myth, and ritual. At the same time, Miss Murdoch's technical, cool interest in the sado-masochism of a man who tries to love his wife's lover, is reinforced by her use of the contrasting Freudian and Sartrean concepts of what the ancient image of the severed head, the Medusa, meant. Freud saw the head as a symbol of male fear of castration, 'the female genitals, feared not desired'. Sartre saw it as an image of the basic fear of being observed. Miss Murdoch plays one off against the other. In this novel it is woolly, greedy, selfish Antonia who holds a watered-down version of the Bloomsbury ethic of loving individuals, which is crushed by the powers of sexual violence as easily as Martin's assumed 'tolerance' of her behaviour. Castration, the voyeuristic witnessing of secret sex, including incest, underlie the plot of this drawing-room comedy, and contribute to its ambiguous elegance. The sexual shifts, the changes of partners, which annoy many of Miss Murdoch's readers, are here part of a stylized fictional representation of the ways in which we are all puppets of blind and incomprehensible forces.

The Unicorn and The Time of the Angels are both, as is made explicit in The Unicorn itself, 'fantasies of the spiritual life'. The good man, the saint or artist, 'nothing himself, lets all things be through him'. Hannah Crean-Smith, the guilty, enclosed 'princess' of The Unicorn, attempts a kind of renunciation of the ego—and ends maybe, with a monstrous sado-masochistic parody of such a renunciation. Carel, the priest of no god, in The Time of the Angels sets out to destroy the fantasies of religion which persist from the days when Christianity was alive: he tries to be 'good for nothing', which not only he, but Miss Murdoch in 'On "God" and "Good"', claim is all that is morally possible in a world where God is dead, and Good an undefinable sense of direction only. He is aware, like his creator, that at the human level life is random and horrible, subject to chance and necessity, without form, without consolation. He creates, therefore for himself, the Nietzschean drama, a high version of the existentialist drama of the lonely, defiant hero. He commits incest with his daughter out of a compulsion

27

which might be part of a Gothic novel, or might be related to Nietzsche's description of Oedipus as the man who had seen the secret of life, 'the horror of nature',[1] the reality of death and the meaninglessness of existence, and who thus knew that all was permitted because all was equally valuable and valueless. In any case, his behaviour, in his attempt to annihilate his ego, is a reinforcement of the sado-masochistic mechanism again. Miss Murdoch is concerned with religious terrors. She is aware, in a way I think no other English novelist is aware, of the importance for our cultural life of the decay of believed Christianity, the loss of a sense of central authority, believed in or opposed. She is aware of the importance of spiritual experience. Various of her characters make sustained attempts at the spiritual life which, with its selflessness, as she says both in *The Bell* and in *The Unicorn*, is not dramatic, and has no story. People have moments of true vision—Effingham, on the point of death in *The Unicorn* sees that love and death are the same, sees the universe flooded with light and meaning because he himself has for a moment been expunged. Carel in *The Time of the Angels* offers the contrary vision, in fact the same, of the true Chaos and Old Night, the vision of the Book of Job that 'there is only power and the marvel of power, there is only chance and the terror of chance'. But neither they, nor the other characters, can live by these visions, and the moment story, drama, action are resumed, so are the psychic mechanisms that pattern them. It is not possible not to have a story. Freud says

> It might be maintained that a case of hysteria is a caricature of a work of art, that an obsessional neurosis is a caricature of a religion, and that a paranoiac delusion is a caricature of a philosophical system.

> (*Totem and Taboo*)

Hannah Crean-Smith's 'religious' behaviour in *The Unicorn* is profoundly ambiguous, but it bears a close resemblance to Freud's description of obsessional neurosis, as the behaviour of her dependants and retainers bears a close resemblance to

[1] See Nietzsche, *The Birth of Tragedy*, which is very illuminating in the context of *The Time of the Angels*.

Freud's quotations in *Totem and Taboo* from Sir James Frazer about the treatment of kings as gods in primitive communities. It is a poetic image, an intellectual game, expressing general truths about human habits and fantasies. (It might be added that the elements of high Gothic[1] in both these novels are part of the same human interest in primitive forces and the forms in which they can be described.)

It might, in this context, also be worth quoting a remark which Iris Murdoch made about the relations of life and myth in a review of Elias Canetti's *Crowds and Power*. 'Canetti has . . . shown, in ways which seem to me entirely fresh, the interaction of the "mythical" with the ordinary stuff of human life. The mythical is not something "extra"; we live in myth and symbol all the time.'[2]

Literature, Miss Murdoch said, was 'a battle between real people and images'. In an interview with Frank Kermode she remarked that she felt her novels 'oscillate rather between attempts to portray a lot of people and giving in to a powerful plot or story'.[3] In those of her later novels where she is attempting psychological realism, free characters, the portraiture of 'a lot of people', she has come to be able to make a very sophisticated use of Shakespeare, both as matter for allusion, and as a source of reference, depth, a real myth of our culture himself. The plots of *The Nice and the Good*, *A Fairly Honourable Defeat*, *The Black Prince*, among others, owe much to him, and what they owe is fascinating and valuable.

There are two excellent reasons for Miss Murdoch's interest in Shakespearean plotting. The first is that she seems to understand, instinctively or as a matter of intellectual decision, that it is a way out of the rather arid English debate about the preservation of the values of nineteenth-century realism against the need to be modern, flexible, innovating,

---

[1] High Gothic—a literary mode, originally very popular in the eighteenth century, which relied on some, or all, of the following constituents: a reference to medieval times, an element of the supernatural, horror, mystery, ruins and haunted castles. It was satirized by Jane Austin in *Northanger Abbey* but has been used, especially by American writers, as a framework for metaphysical speculation and spiritual explanation.

[2] In *The Spectator*, 7 September 1962, pp. 337–8.

[3] Frank Kermode, 'The House of Fiction', p. 64.

not to say experimental. Nathalie Sarraute once remarked that what crushes modern writers is less the sense that their society and situation is incomprehensible than the sense of the weight of their predecessors' achievement, the *use* and exhaustion of the art form by the great writers of the past and the immediate past. In a sense Shakespeare, an eternal part of our culture and mythology, and yet a great technician, is available to learn from in a way that neither George Eliot, nor Forster are. Reading him can be formally exhilarating.

The second reason is an intrinsic part of Iris Murdoch's aesthetic. Shakespeare is the Good, and contemplation of the best is always to be desired.

What Iris Murdoch seems to me technically to have learned from Shakespeare is, again, two things. The first is, as a matter of plotting, that you can have intense realism of character portrayal without having to suppose that this entails *average probability* as part of your structure. Real people may, do, dance in the formal figures of a Shakespearean plot (or indeed, a grotesque Dickensian one) without the sanction of the sense that one is studying a *probable* developing person in a *probable* developing society, which is so necessary to the scientific and sociological beliefs of a George Eliot.

The second is that a very large cast, including a number of peripheral people who are felt to have a life outside the plot, makes for the desiderated 'spread-out substantial picture of the manifold virtues of man and society'. In two radio interviews I had with Iris Murdoch, she returned to Shakespeare's comic people, to Shallow and Silence and the *particularity* of their life, as an example of a moral and aesthetic achievement beyond most of us. In the thirties and forties novelists such as Elizabeth Bowen were placing immense stress on 'relevance'—to plot, to novel-as-a-whole—as a criterion for inclusion in a story. Iris Murdoch has rediscovered the richness of adding apparently gratuitously interesting people and events. These indicate worlds outside the book they are in. (A good example is the strange letters from non-participating people which chatteringly punctuate *An Accidental Man*, offering passion, tragedy, comedy, somewhere between Waugh, Shakespeare and Dickens;

these letters are outside the central plot, but enrich our vision of it.)

In these Shakespearean novels with their huge casts, the central enchanter figures, representing metaphysical powers or truths, are less powerful. Radeechy, whose death and courting of evil in *The Nice and the Good* is a little thing beside the Shakespearean dance of paired lovers, moral mistakes and discoveries, is a poor relation of Carel in *The Time of the Angels*. Julius King, the enchanter, the Prospero, the master of ceremonies in *A Fairly Honourable Defeat* enchants and manipulates both more and less, depending on the moral powers of the people whose lives he touches. He is related to Mischa Fox, in that his rootless violence (he is a germ-war scientist) has its roots in his experiences in Dachau, but his power is less than Mischa's, and the people he meets are denser. He is, like Carel, Nietzschean in his compelling vision of life as a formless joke. Indeed, his relationship with his victim, Rupert, is very like that of Carel with his brother Marcus. Both Rupert and Marcus are writing ethical treatises on Good, on morality in a godless world. Both are unaware of their true dependence on the power of the vanished religion to sustain their hierarchies of value and discrimination. Both are vulnerable to the ruthlessness and violence which mock their morality. But Julius, unlike Carel, does not behave like a Frazerian mythical god-man. He copies the plot of *Much Ado about Nothing*, and like a naturalistic Mephistopheles uses Rupert's own moral blindness and secret complacence to destroy him.

The reason why this novel is in many ways my favourite of Miss Murdoch's later works is because I think, in it, both reader and characters are drawn through the experience of *attention* to the being of others which Miss Murdoch sees as the heart of morality. Julius destroys Rupert. He does not destroy the homosexual marriage of Simon and Axel because, as we are shown, as we experience, they know each other too well. They love each other, talk to each other, consider each other, and reach a breaking-point when they automatically discuss Julius's lies and manipulations for what they are. Just as, in the scene where the black man is being beaten in the restaurant, the characters react typically, morally, entirely convincingly—one is amused (Julius), one intervenes incompetently (Simon), one makes a moral generalization (Axel) and Tallis, who represents Miss Murdoch's new vision of starting from real human needs, as well as the self-denying gentleness that can seem repellent or abstract—Tallis knocks the thugs down. This is a novel in which a patterned plot, the thoughts of the characters, the multiplicity of people, the events, add up to a moral and aesthetic experience both unexpected, delightful and distressing.

At this point it might be worth returning to the critical doubts and debates I discussed briefly in my opening paragraphs. As I hope I have to some extent shown, much of the trouble readers and critics have in responding to, and evaluating Iris Murdoch's novels, is a result of a tension between 'realism' and other more deliberately artificial, even 'experimental' ways of writing in her work. Robert Scholes, in his book *The Fabulators*, includes *The Unicorn* as an example of a new kind of narrative art which returns to older forms of 'fable' rather than following the realist tradition of the novel proper. His other examples are mostly American, and critics who admire the work of such modern American fantasists, or parable writers, as Vonnegut, Hawkes, and Pyncheon have found Iris Murdoch timid or old-fashioned by comparison. Such critics tend to see *Under the Net* as her most successful work, as well as her most original, and her painstaking efforts at creating a fuller and more realistic world in her later books as an aberration, or a retreat into English bourgeois complacencies. Political criticisms have been levelled at her for the increasingly narrow scope of her social world—criticisms that on moral grounds she herself does not feel to be valid. If you are interested in unique individuals, she argues, they can as well be located in the English *haute bourgeoisie* as anywhere.

I would agree, in many ways, that *Under the Net* is aesthetically Iris Murdoch's most satisfying novel: the balance of lucid philosophical debate, lightly but subtly handled emotional pace, and just surrealist fantastic action is new in the English novel and beautifully controlled. *A Severed Head* has the same qualities of delicate control and fusion of several styles and subject matters; drawing-room comedy, shading into French bedroom farce, combined with Jungian psychoanalytic myth and cool philosophical wit. At the other end of the scale, *The Bell* seems to me arguably Miss Murdoch's most successful attempt at realism, emotional and social—the tones of voice of the members of the religious community are beautifully caught, the sexual, aesthetic and religious passions and confusions of the three main characters, Dora, Michael, and, to a lesser extent, Toby, are delicately analysed with the combination of intellectual grasp and sensuous immediacy of George Eliot.

It is, as I have tried to suggest, with those novels in which Iris Murdoch has tried to combine widely differing techniques and narrative methods that confusions arise, sometimes because readers are insufficiently alert and flexible, and sometimes because the writer herself creates jarring effects or difficulties for them. I have suggested, for instance, that *The Time of the Angels* is best read as a mannered philosophical myth, or fantasy, playing games with Nietzsche's *The Birth of Tragedy* and the new school of 'Death of God' theology. The introductory description of the character of Patsy O'Rourke, half-black, half-Irish, however, is written with a clarity, sympathy, density and lack of irony which involve the reader in a way that suggests that the rest of the story will have the emotional immediacy of *The Bell*. Patsy's actions are in fact almost entirely part of Carel's religio-sexual myth (she has to be the Black Madonna to balance the White Virgin Princess, his incestuously seduced daughter Elizabeth). The reader who had responded to that initial description has a right to feel, I think, that the author has promised something she has not performed, whatever the illumination provided by the myth.

In general, Iris Murdoch's careful introductions and histories of her characters are among her best passages of prose, thoughtful, clear, compact—I think of Michael and Dora again, in *The Bell*, of Simon and Axel in *A Fairly Honourable Defeat*, of Hilary Burde in *A Word Child*. Hilary Burde, like Patsy, is a case of a character where a change in both prose style and plotting jars a reader prepared for

33

emotional density and realism. He is, as initially seen, a character created by education, a man made civilized by learning grammar and language to a level of high proficiency, a man of clear mind on a limited front, and violent and ill-comprehended passions. His story, though dramatic, and cleverly related to the story of *Peter Pan*, a recurrent preoccupation of Miss Murdoch's, is not the story of the man we first meet. It is an adventure story, with two accidental deaths and very contrived repeated relationships: it is a Freudian game with incest, with the compulsion to repeat the actions which trap and terrify us. It is rapid, perplexing, funny and terrible. It does not satisfy the realistic expectations aroused by the patient and delicate introductory analysis of the main character.

There is also a problem about Iris Murdoch's use of symbolism, which she herself mocks in *The Black Prince*.[1] This problem arises more with the carefully 'realist' novels than with the more contrived ones: the recurrent images of severed heads, sculpted, dreamed, analysed, in *A Severed Head* work as both joke and myth. The bell itself, in *The Bell*, seems to me the weakest part of a fine novel, because it is so much more patently contrived as a narrative device than either the severed heads or the use of the house, abbey and lake, in *The Bell* itself, to suggest the divisions between conscious and unconscious, secular and spiritual worlds. The bell is an emblem, used as such in the sermons of Michael and James: it is also a crucial actor in the narrative, and, as I have suggested elsewhere,[2] its moment of action, when Dora rings it, is a substitute for a real action, in the real world inhabited by the characters. Dora beats it to 'tell the truth'— but the truth she has to tell has nothing really to do with the bell. The connexion is the novelist's.

The English have arguably never handled the symbolic novel as well as the French, Germans or Americans— Proust's symbols, Thomas Mann's symbols, are woven into the very texture of their prose in a way that neither Lawrence's, Forster's, nor Iris Murdoch's exactly are. In *A Passage to India* Forster made his landscape symbolic and real

[1] See infra., p. 37.

[2] *Degrees of Freedom*, in the chapter on *The Bell* and in the last chapter.

together: Iris Murdoch attempts such a fusion in *The Bell*, with wood, water and abbey. In *Howard's End* and *The Longest Journey* Forster's symbols are rather too deliberately *pointed at* as symbols of England, or social truths (including Howard's End itself). I would argue that this is the case with the roses and painting in that nevertheless excellent novel, *An Unofficial Rose*.

The critic approaching Iris Murdoch's later novels for the first time needs to do so, I think, in the awareness that many serious English novelists are technically moving away from simple realism, from social analysis and precise delineation of the motives and emotions of individuals, to forms much more overtly and deliberately 'unreal'. Not only Iris Murdoch, but Angus Wilson and others are taking an interest in the fairy stories buried in Dickens's plots, in the grotesque caricatures, so like fairy-tale characters, who move amongst Dickens's more 'real' characters. If *The Black Prince* is overtly artificial, drawing attention to its own fictive nature, and to other works of literature in a parodic manner, so are Angus Wilson's two latest novels, *No Laughing Matter* and *As If By Magic*. So, also, are the excellent series of brief novels recently written by Muriel Spark, which call constant attention to the fact that they are just 'stories', fictions, and that that is what is interesting about them. Both Angus Wilson and Iris Murdoch have deep roots in, and strong moral attachments to, the English realist tradition. Both are writing novels which combine old realist morals, and old realist techniques, with a new kind of literary playfulness of which the reader needs to be aware.

I want to end by suggesting that a comparison between Iris Murdoch's first novel, *Under the Net* (1954) and *The Black Prince*, published in 1973, shows a remarkable consistency of themes. These two novels are interesting because both are first-person accounts by men who want to be, or to see themselves as, serious artists, and who are, in this capacity and as lovers, bedevilled by the problems I discussed earlier in this essay—the tension between the attempt to tell, or see, the truth, and the inevitability of fantasy, the need for concepts and form and the recognition that all speech is in a sense distortion, that novelists are fantasy-mongers, and that, as Hugo says in *Under the Net* 'The whole language is a machine for making falsehoods'.

Jake in *Under the Net* has central conversations with Hugo, who holds the view that 'all theorizing is flight. We must be ruled by the situation itself and this is unutterably particular. Indeed, it is something to which we can never get close enough, however hard we may try, as it were, to creep under the net.' (The image of the net comes from Wittgenstein's *Tractatus Logico-Philosophicus* in which he likens our descriptive languages to a mesh put over reality, to map it, and continues that 'Laws, like the law of causation, etc., treat of the network and not what the network describes'.)

In *The Black Prince*, Bradley Pearson, trying to write his *magnum opus*, the story of his love for the daughter of a rival novelist, despairs frequently in the manner of Bledyard in *The Sandcastle* about the impossibility of precise description:

How can one describe a human being 'justly'? How can one describe oneself? With what an air of false coy humility, with what an assumed confiding simplicity one sets about it! 'I am a puritan', and so on. Faugh! How can these statements not be false? Even 'I am tall' has a context. How the angels must laugh and sigh. Yet what can one do but try to lodge one's vision somehow inside this layered stuff of ironic sensibility, which, if I were a fictitious character, would be that much deeper and denser? How prejudiced is this image of Arnold, how superficial this picture of Priscilla! Emotions cloud the view, and so far from isolating the particular, draw generality and even theory in their train.

(*The Black Prince*, pp. 55–6)

Jake has a high sense of difficulty—he has concluded that the present age is not one in which one can write an epic and stopped just short of concluding it was not one in which it was possible to write a novel. He remarks that 'nothing is more paralysing than a sense of historical perspective, especially in literary matters'. He publishes a philosophical dialogue, as does Bradley, who also has a crippling sense of difficulty and the requirements of true excellence. 'Art comes out of endless restraint and silence.' Jake is an unconnected floater, Bradley an income tax inspector who lives austerely waiting for the work of art. But both are prepared to feel gripped and driven by a sense of destiny, of direction, of a source of power, ambivalent to the last, art, love, or fantasy.

Both are measured against prolific apparently 'bad' writers. Jake lives off translating the French Jean-Pierre Breteuil who suddenly turns out to be serious, wins the Prix Goncourt, and imposes on Jake a 'vision of his own destiny' which entails trying to write, whatever the theoretic objections. Bradley has a conversation with his *alter ego*, Arnold Baffin, a prolific writer, whose performance suggests a kind of parody of the unflattering views of Iris Murdoch. Baffin's work is 'A congeries of amusing anecdotes loosely garbled into "racy stories" with the help of half-baked, unmeditated symbolism . . . Arnold Baffin wrote too much, too fast'.

In *Under the Net* it is Jake's experience of his own misprision of people and situations, his own undervaluing of their difference from himself, their complexity, that makes him use concepts, makes him write. Bradley Pearson is invigorated by a contact with the Black Prince, Apollo Loxias, Hamlet, the Love that is the same as Death, the Nietzschean vision which insists that Apollo the Lord of the Muses and Dionysos the god of drunkenness, destruction and chaos are both necessary to art. Bradley is wise and witty in a Murdochian manner about the sado-masochism involved in this vision of art, as he is about his own shortcomings. The fact that these narratives are first-person accounts by intelligent men makes the reading hard, since the narrator's illusions are refined illusions. In *The Black Prince*, Miss Murdoch comically layers this difficulty with references to Bradley's own fictionality, to the idea that both he and Apollo might be 'the invention of a minor novelist', and with other, partial, accounts of the plot by other characters. Yet Bradley says much that she has said herself, *in propria persona*, and is clearly, among other things, an authorial joke about the relations of author and character. It is in this context that Bradley's description of Shakespeare's achievement in *Hamlet* becomes fascinating from the point of view of Miss Murdoch's work. She believes, she has said, that the self of the artist should be expunged from this work, that Shakespeare's greatness is his anonymity. Yet she recognizes, in the Sonnets and in *Hamlet* a kind of 'self' which Bradley discusses in this speech.

Shakespeare, he says 'is speaking as few artists can speak, in the first person and yet at the pinnacle of artifice . . . Shakespeare here makes the crisis of his own identity into the very central stuff of his art. He transmutes his private obsessions into a rhetoric so public that it can be mumbled by any child. He enacts the purification of speech, and yet this is something comic, a sort of trick, like a huge pun, like a long almost pointless joke.'

'*Hamlet* is words, and so is Hamlet'.[1]

In a sense, here, we have another version of Miss Murdoch's 'Good' which is virtually impossible to attain—the complete creation of a character in *words*, using the writer, but *for* the language. It is an extraordinary example of one of the high moments of art where there is no contradiction between words and things, between men and the images of men. But it is also, as Miss Murdoch and *her* character point out, endlessly comic. And Miss Murdoch's novel conducts a comic joke, itself, around the vision of *Hamlet*. 'All novels' she once claimed, 'are necessarily comic', just as her Apollo claims, in his epilogue, 'all human beings are figures of fun. Art celebrates this. Art is adventure stories'. Another thing for which one increasingly admires Miss Murdoch is aesthetic courage: knowing, better than most writers, the historical difficulties of writing good novels now, the moral difficulties of writing good novels at all, she continues to produce comic metaphysical adventures of a high order. What Arnold Baffin did not say, but might have said, in his quarrel with Bradley Pearson about being an 'artist' and being a 'professional writer' is that Shakespeare was both of these, too.

---

[1] *The Black Prince*, pp. 161 et seq.

IRIS MURDOCH

A Select Bibliography

(Place of publication London, unless stated otherwise)

Bibliography:

'Criticism of Iris Murdoch: A Selected Checklist', by Ann Culley with John Feaster, *Modern Fiction Studies*, XV, iii, Autumn 1969, 449–57
—Iris Murdoch Special Number. This bibliography lists works by and about Iris Murdoch, including selected reviews of the novels.
'An Iris Murdoch Checklist', by R. L. Widmann, *Critique: Studies in Modern Fiction*, X, 1967, 17–29
—including a fuller list of reviews.

Works:

SARTRE, ROMANTIC RATIONALIST (1953). *Philosophy and literary criticism*
UNDER THE NET (1954). *Fiction*
THE FLIGHT FROM THE ENCHANTER (1956). *Fiction*
THE SANDCASTLE (1957). *Fiction*
THE BELL (1958). *Fiction*
A SEVERED HEAD (1961). *Fiction*
AN UNOFFICIAL ROSE (1962). *Fiction*
THE UNICORN (1963). *Fiction*
THE ITALIAN GIRL (1964). *Fiction*
THE RED AND THE GREEN (1965). *Historical Fiction*
THE TIME OF THE ANGELS (1966). *Fiction*
THE NICE AND THE GOOD (1968). *Fiction*
BRUNO'S DREAM (1969). *Fiction*
THE SOVEREIGNTY OF GOOD (1970). *Philosophy*
—contains three previously published philosophical papers. 'The Idea of Perfection' from *Yale Review*, 1964; 'The Sovereignty of Good over other Concepts' (Leslie Stephen Lecture, 1967) and 'On "God" and "Good"' from *The Anatomy of Knowledge*, Routledge & Kegan Paul, 1969.
A FAIRLY HONOURABLE DEFEAT (1970). *Fiction*
AN ACCIDENTAL MAN (1971). *Fiction*
THE BLACK PRINCE (1973). *Fiction*
THREE ARROWS and THE SERVANTS IN THE SNOW (1973). *Plays*
THE SACRED AND PROFANE LOVE MACHINE (1974). *Fiction*
A WORD CHILD (1975). *Fiction*
HENRY AND CATO (1976). *Fiction*

Articles:

'The Novelist as Metaphysician', *The Listener*, XLIII, 16 March 1950, 473, 476.

'The Existentialist Hero', *The Listener*, XLIII, 23 March 1950, 523–4.

'Nostalgia for the Particular', *Proceedings of the Aristotelian Society*, —*Dreams and Self-Knowledge*, Supp. Vol. XXX, 1956.

'Knowing the Void', *The Spectator*, CXCVII, 2 November 1956, 613–14.

'Metaphysics and Ethics'. In: *The Nature of Metaphysics*, ed. D. F. Pears (1957).

'Hegel in Modern Dress, *New Statesman*, 53, 25 May 1957, 675.

'T. S. Eliot as a Moralist'. In: *T. S. Eliot: A Symposium for his Seventieth Birthday*, ed. Neville Braybrooke (1958).

'A House of Theory', *Partisan Review*, XXVI, 1959, 17–31 —also in *Conviction*, ed. *Norman Mackenzie*, 1958.

'The Sublime and the Beautiful Revisited', *Yale Review*, XLIX, 1959, 242–71.

'The Sublime and the Good', *Chicago Review*, XIII, Autumn 1959, 42–55.

'Against Dryness', *Encounter*, XVI, January 1961, 16–20.

'Mass, Might and Myth', *The Spectator*, CCIX, 7 September 1962, 337–8.

'Speaking of Writing', *The Times*, 13 February 1964, 5.

'The Darkness of Practical Reason', *Encounter*, XXVII, July 1966, 46–50.

'Existentialists and Mystics'. In: *Essays and Poems presented to Lord David Cecil*, ed. W. W. Robson (1970).

Critical Studies:

THE ANGRY DECADE: A Survey of the Cultural Revolt of the Nineteen-Fifties, by Kenneth Allsopp (1958).

'Iris Murdoch: The Solidity of the Normal', by G. S. Fraser, *International Literary Annual* II, ed. John Wain 1959.

'Iris Murdoch and the Romantic Novel', by Gabriel Pearson, *New Left Review*, XIII-XIV, January–April 1962, 137–45.

'Iris Murdoch's *Under the Net*', by Malcolm Bradbury, *Critical Quarterly*, No. 4, Spring 1962.

'Symbol as Narrative Device', by Jacques Souvage, *English Studies*, XLIII, 2, April 1962.

THE NEW UNIVERSITY WITS AND THE END OF MODERNISM, by William Van O'Connor (1963) —contains an essay on 'Iris Murdoch: The Formal and the Contingent'.

'Iris Murdoch and the Symbolist Novel', by Graham Martin, *British Journal of Aesthetics*, V, July 1965, 296–300.

DEGREES OF FREEDOM, by A. S. Byatt (1965).

THE DISCIPLINED HEART, by Peter Wolfe (1966)
—contains useful information but some very odd interpretations of the moral structure of the novels themselves.

THE FABULATORS, by Robert Scholes (1967)
—contains an essay on *The Unicorn* as fable.

IRIS MURDOCH, by Rubin Rabinovitz; New York (1968)
—Columbia Essays on Modern Writers, No. 34.

THE CHARACTERS OF LOVE: A Study in the Literature of Personality, by John Bayley (1968).

'Allusions in the Early Novels of Iris Murdoch', by Howard German, *Modern Fiction Studies*, XV, Autumn 1969, 361–77.

'The Fight against Fantasy: Iris Murdoch's *The Red and the Green*', by Peter Kemp, *Modern Fiction Studies*, XV, Autumn 1969, 403–15.

'The Mythic History of *A Severed Head*', by Alice P. Kenney, *Modern Fiction Studies*, XV, Autumn 1969, 387–401.

'The Range of Allusion in the Novels of Iris Murdoch', by Howard German, *Journal of Modern Literature*, 1971.

MODERN ESSAYS, by Frank Kermode (1971).

'Shakespearean Allusions in *A Fairly Honourable Defeat*' by Robert Hoskins, *Twentieth Century Literature*, 1972.

POSSIBILITIES: Essays on the State of the Novel, by Malcolm Bradbury (1973)
—a very illuminating essay, extending his earlier work on *Under the Net*.

UNOFFICIAL SELVES, by Patrick Swinden (1973)
—generally pursuing Iris Murdoch's ideas about character; good on *A Fairly Honourable Defeat* in particular.

Note:

There is a great deal of periodical literature, much of it wild academic symbol-hunting, or simple reiteration of Miss Murdoch's own writings. Serious students should consult the *Modern Fiction Studies* bibliography mentioned above.

Interviews:

'House of Fiction: Interviews with Seven English Novelists', *Partisan Review*, XXX, 1963, 61–82
—interview with Frank Kermode.

Interview with Peter Orr, recorded 27 May 1965, British Council, London.

'An Exclusive Interview', *Books and Bookmen*, XI, September 1966
—interview with Stephanie Nettell.
'An interview with Iris Murdoch', *London Magazine*, VIII, June 1968,
    59–73
—interview with W. K. Rose; also in *Shenandoah* XIX, Winter 1968.
Interview recorded in March 1968, part reproduced in *The Listener*,
    LXXIX, 4 April 1968
—with Ronald Bryden and A. S. Byatt.
Forty-minute taped interview, recorded 26 October 1971, BBC
    Archives
—interview with A. S. Byatt.
'Iris Murdoch in conversation with Malcolm Bradbury', recorded 27
    February 1976, British Council Tape No. RS 2001.

WRITERS AND THEIR WORK

SMART: Geoffrey Grigson
SMOLLETT: Laurence Brander
STEELE, ADDISON: A. R. Humphreys
STERNE: D. W. Jefferson
SWIFT: J. Middleton Murry (1955)
SWIFT: A. Norman Jeffares (1976)
VANBRUGH: Bernard Harris
HORACE WALPOLE: Hugh Honour

Nineteenth Century:
ARNOLD: Kenneth Allott
AUSTEN: S. Townsend Warner (1951)
AUSTEN: B. C. Southam (1975)
BAGEHOT: N. St John-Stevas
THE BRONTË SISTERS:
           Phyllis Bentley (1950)
THE BRONTËS: I & II: Winifred Gérin
E. B. BROWNING: Alethea Hayter
ROBERT BROWNING: John Bryson
SAMUEL BUTLER: G. D. H. Cole
BYRON: I, II & III: Bernard Blackstone
CARLYLE: David Gascoyne
CARROLL: Derek Hudson
CLOUGH: Isobel Armstrong
COLERIDGE: Kathleen Raine
CREEVEY & GREVILLE: J. Richardson
DE QUINCEY: Hugh Sykes Davies
DICKENS: K. J. Fielding
   EARLY NOVELS: Trevor Blount
   LATER NOVELS: Barbara Hardy
DISRAELI: Paul Bloomfield
GEORGE ELIOT: Lettice Cooper
FITZGERALD: Joanna Richardson
GASKELL: Miriam Allott
GISSING: A. C. Ward
HARDY: R. A. Scott-James
         and C. Day Lewis
HAZLITT: J. B. Priestley
HOOD: Laurence Brander
HOPKINS: Geoffrey Grigson
T. H. HUXLEY: William Irvine
KEATS: Edmund Blunden
LAMB: Edmund Blunden
LANDOR: G. Rostrevor Hamilton
LEAR: Joanna Richardson
MACAULAY: G. R. Potter
MEREDITH: Phyllis Bartlett
MILL: Maurice Cranston

MORRIS: Philip Henderson
NEWMAN: J. M. Cameron
PATER: Ian Fletcher
PEACOCK: J. I. M. Stewart
CHRISTINA ROSSETTI: G. Battiscombe
D. G. ROSSETTI: Oswald Doughty
RUSKIN: Peter Quennell
SCOTT: Ian Jack
SHELLEY: G. M. Matthews
SOUTHEY: Geoffrey Carnall
STEPHEN: Phyllis Grosskurth
STEVENSON: G. B. Stern
SWINBURNE: Ian Fletcher
TENNYSON: B. C. Southam
THACKERAY: Laurence Brander
FRANCIS THOMPSON: Peter Butter
TROLLOPE: Hugh Sykes Davies
WILDE: James Laver
WORDSWORTH: Helen Darbishire

Twentieth Century:
ACHEBE: A. Ravenscroft
ARDEN: Glenda Leeming
AUDEN: Richard Hoggart
BECKETT: J-J. Mayoux
BELLOC: Renée Haynes
BENNETT: Frank Swinnerton (1950)
BENNETT: Kenneth Young (1975)
BETJEMAN: John Press
BLUNDEN: Alec M. Hardie
BOND: Simon Trussler
BRIDGES: John Sparrow
BURGESS: Carol M. Dix
CAMPBELL: David Wright
CARY: Walter Allen
CHESTERTON: C. Hollis
CHURCHILL: John Connell
COLLINGWOOD: E. W. F. Tomlin
COMPTON-BURNETT: R. Glynn Grylls
CONRAD: Oliver Warner
DE LA MARE: Kenneth Hopkins
NORMAN DOUGLAS: Ian Greenlees
LAWRENCE DURRELL: G. S. Fraser
T. S. ELIOT: M. C. Bradbrook
T. S. ELIOT: The Making of
   'The Waste Land': M. C. Bradbrook
FORD MADOX FORD: Kenneth Young
FORSTER: Rex Warner